Popular Music Theory

Preliminary Grade

by

Camilla Sheldon & Tony Skinner

A CIP record for this publication is available from the British Library.

ISBN: 1-898466-40-8

First edition © 2001 and 2004 Registry Publications Ltd.

Published in Great Britain by

Registry Mews, 11 to 13 Wilton Road, Bexhill, E. Sussex, TN40 1HY

Typesetting by

Take Note Publishing Limited, Lingfield, Surrey

Instrument photographs supplied by John Hornby Skewes Ltd.

Printed in Great Britain.

Contents

Introduction

This book covers all the material you need to know to take the London College of Music Preliminary Grade examination in Popular Music Theory.

As well as helping you to pass the examination, the intention of this book is to introduce and explain the theory behind popular music and so help you improve your musicianship. You can benefit from working through the book whether or not you intend to take an examination. You will benefit most if you try out the information you learn in this book in a practical music-making setting, by relating the information to your instrument and by using it to create your own music.

This book is part of a series that offers a structured and progressive approach to understanding the theory of popular music and whilst it can be used for independent study, it is ideally intended as a supplement to group or individual tuition.

The book begins with a brief guide explaining the basics of music notation. It is essential that you study this section before proceeding with the rest of the book.

The chapters of the book reflect the sections of the examination. Each chapter outlines the facts you need to know for the examination, together with the theory behind the facts. Each chapter is completed with some examples of the types of questions that will appear in the examination paper. The sample questions are intended to give a clear guide as to the types of questions that may be asked in the examination, however the list of questions is neither exclusive nor exhaustive. Once you have worked through the questions at the end of each section you can check your answers by looking at the 'Sample Answers' in the back of the book.

Examinations are held twice a year and you can only enter for an examination by completing the stamped entry form at the back of each handbook.

We hope you enjoy working through this book and wish you success with the examination and all your musical endeavours.

Camilla Sheldon and Tony Skinner

Music notation is normally written on five lines that are known as a *staff* (or *stave*). Each line, and each space between the lines, represents a different note. When you write music notation you have to be very careful that the noteheads are either dissected by a line, or are placed in the space between two lines.

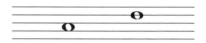

clefs

A *clef* is the symbol that tells you which notes are represented by the different lines and spaces.

 The *treble clef* (or *G clef*) tells you that the second line from the bottom is G.

 The *bass clef* (or *F clef*) tells you that the second line from the top is F.

All other notes progress in alphabetical order up and down each staff from these notes.

Temporary extra lines, known as leger lines, are used for any notes that are either too high or too low for a staff.

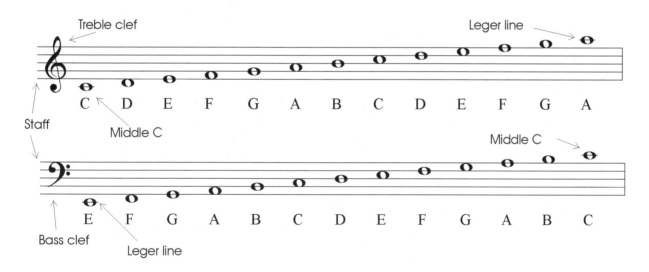

When writing a treble clef ensure that it curls around the G line.

When writing a bass clef ensure that you add a dot on either side of the F line.

notes

It is useful to have a few (mnemonic) phrases to help you remember the names of the notes on the clefs. Sometimes the sillier the phrases are, the easier they are to remember. Here are a few we've made up with a 'wild animal' theme, but you might remember the notes even better if you make up your own unique phrases.

Lines in the treble clef
Eager Giraffes Bathe During February

Spaces in the treble clef
Fast Antelopes Can Escape

Lines in the bass clef
Grizzly Bears Don't Fear Anyone

Spaces in the bass clef
Angry Cheetahs Emerge Growling

sharps

Between most letter names there is a *whole step* (or *whole tone*). For example, the distance between the notes A and B is a whole step. However, you can also move just a *half step* (or *semitone*) up from any note by using signs known as *sharps* (#). For example, the note a half step above F is F sharp (F#). So F# is halfway between F and G.

There is a sharp note between most letter name notes. The exceptions are between E and F, and between B and C. There is only a half step between these two sets of notes and so no sharps exist between them. If you look at the diagram of the piano keyboard below you will notice that there are no (sharp) notes between E and F, and between B and C.

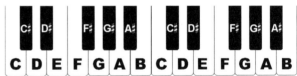

Therefore, the order of notes in the musical alphabet progresses like this:

A A# B C C# D D# E F F# G G#

When you write sharp notes on the staff, the # sign must be written to the left of the notehead. Depending upon the note, the middle of the # sign should be either dissected by the same line as the notehead, or placed in the same space as the notehead. When a sharp is written before a note it is called an *accidental*. Here is an example of F# written in both the treble and bass clefs.

key signatures

If a piece of music always uses an F# rather than an F, instead of writing the # every time the note occurs, the music is given a *key signature*. The # sign is written across the F line, immediately after the clef, at the start of every staff of music. This means that all the F notes are now F#.

stems

Half notes (*minims*) and *quarter notes* (*crotchets*) are written with a thin vertical line attached to the notehead. This is called a *stem*. It is important to write it in the correct direction. In simple melodies, stems go 'up on the right' if the note is below the middle line of the staff, and 'down on the left' if the note is above the middle line on the staff. The stems of notes on the middle line can go either way, depending upon the direction of the adjacent notes in the rest of the bar. Stems should be about the height of a staff in length.

musical terms

Sometimes there are two different names that can be used for the same musical elements. Also, the terminology that is widely used in N. America (and increasingly amongst pop, rock and jazz musicians in the U.K. and elsewhere) is different to that traditionally used in the U.K. and other parts of the world.

A summary of the main alternative terms is shown below. In the examination you can use either version.

whole note	=	semibreve
half note	=	minim
quarter note	=	crotchet
whole step	=	whole tone
half step	=	semitone
staff	=	stave
measures	=	bars
keynote	=	tonic
$\frac{4}{4}$	=	𝄴
leger line	=	ledger line
treble clef	=	G clef
bass clef	=	F clef

Use this space to write yourself some 'reminders' about the important points of music notation...

Section One – scales and keys

In this section of the exam you will be asked to write out and identify some of the following scales and keys signatures:

- C major
- G major
- A natural minor
- E natural minor

So that the scales learnt in theory can be used effectively in a practical way, you should be able to do the following:

- Write out, and identify, the *letter names* that make up each scale.
- Write out, and identify, each scale in standard *music notation* (adding or identifying the key signature where appropriate). You can write your answer in either the treble clef or the bass clef.
- Write out, and identify, the *degrees* of each scale.

the theory

scales

A *scale* is a series of notes that are arranged in a specific order from the lowest note to the highest note. The note that is lowest in pitch is the first note of a scale. This note is also the one that sounds the strongest and is called the *keynote* (or *tonic*). The last note of the scale is the same as the first, but higher, and is known as the *octave*.

Scales can be played ascending or descending, and notes from scales are used for writing melodies or for improvising.

major and natural minor

Major and natural minor scales are constructed using a combination of *whole steps* (also known as *whole tones*) and *half steps* (also known as *semitones*).

- A half step (H) is the distance from one note to the closest note above (or below) it, for example from F# to G.
- A whole step (W), for example from F to G, is double the distance of a half step; so a whole step is the equivalent of two half steps.

Major scales are constructed using the pattern of whole and half steps shown below:

$$\boxed{\text{W W H W W W H}}$$

The C major scale, for example, is constructed in the following way:

- C to the 2nd note (D) = whole step
- D to the 3rd note (E) = whole step
- E to the 4th note (F) = half step*
- F to the 5th note (G) = whole step
- G to the 6th note (A) = whole step
- A to the 7th note (B) = whole step
- B to the octave (C) = half step*

* Remember, that because there are no sharps between B and C, and between E and F, the gap within each of these pairs of notes is only a half step.

If you memorise the major scale 'step-pattern' (W W H W W W H) you will always be able to find out which notes make up any of the major scales. Simply start with the keynote and then use the step-pattern to find the other notes – making sure that, apart from the keynote and octave, each letter name is only used once. For example:

G major scale

notes: G A B C D E F# G
pattern: W W H W W W H

Natural minor scales are constructed using a different step-pattern to major scales. The step-pattern for natural minor scales is:

$$\boxed{\text{W H W W H W W}}$$

(Note that this is the same step-pattern as if the major scale had started on its sixth note.)

The A natural minor scale, for example, is constructed as follows:

- A to the 2nd note (B) = whole step
- B to the 3rd note (C) = half step
- C to the 4th note (D) = whole step
- D to the 5th note (E) = whole step
- E to the 6th note (F) = half step
- F to the 7th note (G) = whole step
- G to the octave (A) = whole step

If you memorise this pattern (W H W W H W W) you will always be able to find out which notes make up any of the natural minor scales. Simply start with the keynote and then use the step-pattern to find the other notes – making sure that, apart from the keynote and octave, each letter name is only used once. For example:

E natural minor scale

notes: E F# G A B C D E
pattern: W H W W H W W

scale notes

Here are the names of the notes contained within the major and natural minor scales that are required for the Preliminary Grade exam.

C major:	C D E F G A B C
G major:	G A B C D E F♯ G
A natural minor:	A B C D E F G A
E natural minor:	E F♯ G A B C D E

You should try and play these scales on your instrument so that you can hear the sound of them. Playing them will also help you to memorise the notes that make up each scale. If you forget the names of the notes in these scales, you can work them out in the following way:

1. Use the 'step-pattern'

   W W H W W W H

   to work out the notes of any major scale.

2. Use the 'step-pattern'

   W H W W H W W

   to work out the notes of any natural minor scale.

When working out the notes in any scale, remember that because there are no sharps between B and C, and between E and F, the gap within each of these pairs of notes is only a half step.

keys and key signatures

The *key* that a song is in determines the song's overall sound, known as its *tonality*. The key also determines which scale (and therefore which notes) will normally be used to make up the melody of that song. For example, if a tune is written in the key of G major it is likely to use notes from the G major scale. Because the keynote is the strongest note many tunes will begin and/or end with it.

A *key signature* tells you which key a piece of music is written in. In music notation *key signatures* are written, immediately after the clef, at the start of the music, and are repeated on every new staff of music.

Here are the key signatures for the scales set for the Preliminary Grade exam.

G major and E natural minor.

These two scales share the same key signature: one sharp, F#.

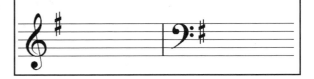

C major and A natural minor.

These two scales share the same key signature: no sharps or flats. So, in this instance, the key signature is effectively blank.

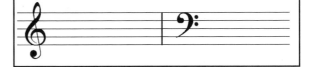

---

scale notation

Here are the scales required for Preliminary Grade written out in both the treble clef and the bass clef:

C major

G major

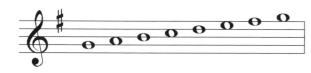

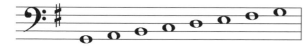

A natural minor

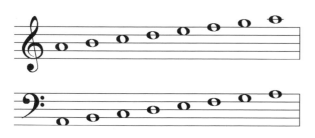

E natural minor

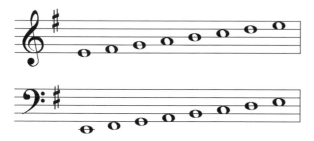

Notice that, in both the G major and E natural minor scales, there is no need to put a # before the F note: as the F# is included in the key signature all F notes automatically become F#.

scale degrees

In popular music, instead of using the letter names of the notes in a scale, musicians often use numbers. Each note of the scale is given a number, referring to its scale degree, starting with the keynote as '1'. For example, in the C major scale the notes are numbered as follows:

C	D	E	F	G	A	B	C
1	2	3	4	5	6	7	8

So, rather than talking about the G note in the scale of C, pop musicians might refer to it as the 5th degree of the scale.

Here are all the other scales set for Preliminary Grade:

Scale / degree:	1	2	3	4	5	6	7	8
G major:	G	A	B	C	D	E	F♯	G
A natural minor:	A	B	C	D	E	F	G	A
E natural minor:	E	F♯	G	A	B	C	D	E

Below are some examples of the types of questions that candidates may be asked in this section of the exam. If you can't answer a question, then carefully re-read the preceding chapter and the 'Guide To Music Notation' at the front of the book.

When answering questions that involve writing scales in notation, you can choose to write them in either the treble or bass clef. Either way, you need only write them ascending using whole notes (as shown here).

Q1. Which scale contains the notes
    G A B C D E F# G ?   A1. _____

Q2. Write the notes of the A natural
    minor scale using letter names.   A2. _____

Q3. Write the notes of the E natural
    minor scale using letter names.   A3. _____

Q4. Write the notes of the C major
    scale using letter names.   A4. _____

Q5. Name the major scale
    that has this key signature.   A5. _____

Q6. Which scale is this?

                                          A6. _____

                                          A7.
Q7. Write one octave of the A natural   _____
    minor scale in either the treble or   _____
    bass clef.   _____
                                          _____

Q8. Which note occurs on the 6th
    degree of the E natural minor
    scale?   A8. _____

Q9. On which degree of the G major
    scale does the note C occur?   A9. _____

Section Two – chords

In this section of the exam you will be asked to write out and identify some of the following chords:

- C major
- G major
- A minor
- E minor

So that the chords learnt in theory can be used effectively in a practical way, you should be able to do the following:

- Use *chord symbols* to identify the chords.
- Write out, and identify, the *letter names* and *scale degrees* that make up each chord.
- Write out, and identify, each chord in standard *music notation*. You can write your answer in either the treble clef or the bass clef.

the theory

chords

A *chord* is a collection of two or more notes that are sounded together. Chords can be used to accompany melodies or as backings for improvisation.

Three note chords are known as *triads*. The 1st note of a chord (i.e. the note that gives the chord its name) is called the *root note*.

The 1st, 3rd, and 5th notes of the major scale make up a major triad.

C major scale		C major triad		G major scale		G major triad
C	→	C		G	→	G
D				A		
E	→	E		B	→	B
F				C		
G	→	G		D	→	D
A				E		
B				F#		
C				G		

The 1st, 3rd, and 5th notes of the natural minor scale make up a minor triad.

A natural minor scale		A minor triad
A	→	A
B		
C	→	C
D		
E	→	E
F		
G		
A		

E natural minor scale		E minor triad
E	→	E
F#		
G	→	G
A		
B	→	B
C		
D		
E		

chord symbols

The symbol for a major triad is the capital letter of the name of the chord; so the symbol for the C major triad is C, and the symbol for the G major triad is G.

The symbol for a minor triad is the capital letter of the name of the chord plus lower case 'm'; so the symbol for the A minor triad is Am, and the symbol for the E minor triad is Em.

Chord name	Symbol
C major	C
G major	G
A minor	Am
E minor	Em

Minor triads can sometimes be seen written like this: Ami, Emi. Or like this: A-, E-.

notes in chords

Here are the names of the notes contained within each chord. These are known as *chord tones*.

C:	C	E	G
G:	G	B	D
Am:	A	C	E
Em:	E	G	B

You can work out the names of the notes within the chords on your own by first working out the relevant major or natural minor scale with the same keynote, and then selecting the 1st, 3rd and 5th notes of that scale to form the chord. For example, to find the notes in the C major triad, first work out the notes in the C major scale (refer to the previous chapter if you are unsure how to do this) and then select the 1st, 3rd and 5th notes of this scale to form the C major triad.

chord notation

Here are the four chords written out in both the treble clef and the bass clef:

C

G

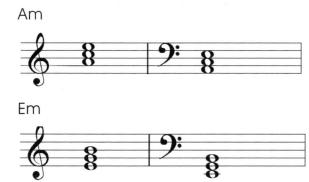

Am

Em

Notice that, in all major and minor triads, if the root note of the chord is on a line then the remaining notes of the triad occur on the two lines above, whereas if the root note of the chord is in a space then the remaining notes of the triad occur in the two spaces above.

scale degrees

In the same way that pop musicians often use numbers to talk about the notes in a scale, they sometimes use numbers to talk about the notes in a chord. Each note in the chord is given a number that refers to the *scale degree* from which that note is taken.

For example, the C major triad is numbered as shown below because it contains the first, third and fifth notes of the C major scale.

C E G

1 3 5

In this example, rather than talking about the E note in the chord of C major, pop musicians might refer to it as 'the 3rd of the chord' because it is the same note as the 3rd degree of the C major scale.

All major and minor triads contain the 1st, 3rd and 5th notes of the major or natural minor scale with the same keynote.

	1	2	3	4	5	6	7	8
C major scale	1	2	3 ⌢ 4		5	6	7 ⌢ 8	
	C	D	E	F	G	A	B	C
C major triad	1		3		5			
G major scale	1	2	3	4	5	6	7	8
	G	A	B	C	D	E	F#	G
G major triad	1		3		5			
A natural minor scale	1	2	3	4	5	6	7	8
	A	B	C	D	E	F	G	A
A minor triad	1		3		5			
E natural minor scale	1	2	3	4	5	6	7	8
	E	F#	G	A	B	C	D	E
E minor triad	1		3		5			

Remember that the 1st note of any scale is known as the *keynote* (or *tonic*), whilst the 1st note of any chord (i.e. the note that gives the chord its pitch name) is known as the *root*.

the exam

Below are some examples of the types of questions that candidates may be asked in this section of the exam. If you can't answer a question, then carefully re-read the preceding chapter and the 'Guide to Music Notation' at the front of the book.

When answering questions that involve writing chords in notation, you can choose to write your answers in either the treble clef or the bass clef. You should place the notes of each chord vertically on top of one another, using whole notes (as shown in the example here). The notes of each chord should be written in *root position*, that means put the root note at the bottom, then write the third note and finally the fifth.

Q1. Which triad contains the notes
G   B   D?   A1. _____

Q2. Write the notes of the Am triad
using letter names.   A2. _____

Q3. Write the notes of the C triad using
letter names.   A3. _____

Q4. Which chord is this?
                                    A4. _____

Q5. Write out the Em triad in either the   A5. _____
treble clef or bass clef.

Q6. Name the root and the fifth of the
E minor triad.   A6. Root: _____ Fifth: _____

Q7. B is the third of which major triad,
C major or G major?   A7. _____

Section Three – rhythm notation

In this section of the exam you will be asked to write out and identify some of the following note and rest values:

- whole notes (semibreves)
- half notes (minims)
- quarter notes (crotchets)

- whole rests (semibreve rests)
- half rests (minim rests)
- quarter rests (crotchet rests)

You will also be asked to use these notes and rests in $\frac{4}{4}$ time.

So that the rhythm notation learnt in theory can be used effectively in a practical way, you should be able to do the following:

- Write out, and identify, the symbols for the note and rest values listed above.
- Identify the values of different notes and rests.
- Explain how notes and rests of different values fit into bars (measures) of $\frac{4}{4}$ time.
- Group notes and rests correctly within $\frac{4}{4}$ time.
- Compose simple rhythms in $\frac{4}{4}$ time using the note and rest values listed.

the theory

note and rest values

All music has a pulse or beat. In popular music this is usually clearly defined by the rhythm section (drums, bass, rhythm guitar, percussion). The rhythm of a piece of music is described and written down by using notes and rests. The type of note used tells you how many beats a sound lasts for, whilst a rest tells you how many beats a silence lasts for. Below are the names of the different types of notes and rests required for the Preliminary Grade exam, the symbols for them and how many beats each type of note and rest lasts for in $\frac{4}{4}$ time.

name	note	rest	duration
quarter note (or crotchet)			1 beat
half note (or minim)			2 beats
whole note (or semibreve)			4 beats

The diagram below shows the relative value of each type of note:

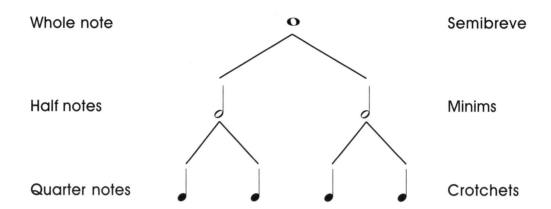

Whole note		Semibreve
Half notes		Minims
Quarter notes		Crotchets

time signatures

Not all beats in music sound exactly the same – some beats (often the first of every four) are stronger than others. This accenting of certain beats divides music up into small sections that are known as *bars* (or *measures*).

A *time signature*, which is written once at the beginning of a piece of music, shows how many beats there are in each bar, and what type of note represents a beat. The top number shows the number of beats per bar, whilst the bottom number shows the type of note which represents a beat.

For example, a $\frac{4}{4}$ time signature tells you that there are four quarter note (crotchet) beats in each bar.

The 4 at the top means that there are four beats in the bar.

The 4 at the bottom means that each beat is a quarter note.

$\frac{4}{4}$ time can also be indicated by a **C**

---

writing tips

- When writing a time signature, the tip of the top number should touch the top line of the staff, and the base of the bottom number should touch the bottom line of the staff.

- The time signature should always be written after the clef and the key signature.

- The time signature should only be written in the first bar of a piece of music – it does not need to be repeated on each staff of music.

---

grouping of notes and rests

In $\frac{4}{4}$ time each bar must add up to the equivalent of four quarter note beats, whatever the combination of note and rest values. For example:

There are rules about how combinations of these notes can be written. At this level you should be aware of the following rule:

You can write a half rest (minim rest) in the first half of the bar (on beats one and two) or in the second half of the bar (on beats three and four). However, you should not write a half rest in the middle of the bar (on beats two and three) – instead you should use two quarter rests.

This rule exists in music notation so that all four beats of the bar can be clearly identified. Writing music this way makes it easier to read.

This is correct.

This is *incorrect.*

---

writing tips

Take care to write the symbols for rests correctly.

The quarter rest begins in the top space and ends in the bottom space of the staff.

The half rest sits on the middle line of the staff.

The whole rest hangs from the second highest line of the staff.

the exam

Below are some examples of the types of questions that candidates may be asked in this section of the exam. If you can't answer a question, then carefully re-read the preceding chapter and the 'Guide To Music Notation' at the front of the book.

Q1. What type of note is this?

A1. _____

Q2. What type of note is this?

A2. _____

A3.
_____

Q3. Write the symbol for a half note (minim) at a pitch of your choice. Use either the treble or bass clef.

Q4. Write the symbol for a half rest (minim rest).

A4.

Q5. What type of rest is this?

A5. _____

Q6. How many of this type of note are needed to fill a bar of $\frac{4}{4}$ time?

A6. _____

Q7. Using a clef and note of your choice, write two different bars of rhythm in $\frac{4}{4}$ time, using only half notes (minims) and quarter notes (crotchets).

A7.

Q8. Complete the bars by inserting the appropriate rest or rests in the spaces marked *.

A8.

Section Four – sample answers

Section One – scales and keys [Max. 45 marks]

A1.   G major

A2.   A B C D E F G A

A3.   E F# G A B C D E

A4.   C D E F G A B C

A5.   G major

A6.   C major

A7.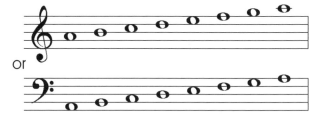

A8.   C

A9.   4th

Section Two – chords [Max. 35 marks]

A1.   G major

A2.   A C E

A3.   C E G

A4.   C major

A5.

A6.   Root: E.   Fifth: B.

A7.   G major

Section Three – rhythm notation   [Max. 20 marks]

A1.   Quarter note (or crotchet)

A2.   Whole note (or semibreve)

A3.

A4.

A5.   Whole rest (or semibreve rest).

A6.   Four

A7.

A8.

Examination Entry Form
Popular Music Theory

PRELIMINARY GRADE ONLY

PLEASE COMPLETE CLEARLY USING BLOCK CAPITAL LETTERS

SESSION (Summer/Winter): _____ YEAR: _____

Preferred Examination Centre (if known): _____
If left blank, you will be examined at the nearest examination centre to your home address.

Candidate Details:

Candidate Name (as to appear on certificate):

_____

Address: _____

_____

_____ Postcode: _____

Tel. No. (day): _____ (evening): _____

Teacher Details:

Teacher Name (as to appear on certificate): _____

Registry Tutor Code (if applicable): _____

Address: _____

_____ Postcode: _____

Tel. No. (day): _____ (evening): _____

The standard LCM Exams entry form is NOT valid for Popular Music Theory entries. Entry to the examination is only possible via this original form.

Photocopies of this form will not be accepted under *any* circumstances.

IMPORTANT NOTES

- It is the candidate's responsibility to have knowledge of, and comply with, the current syllabus requirements. Where candidates are entered for examinations by teachers, the teacher must take responsibility that candidates are entered in accordance with the current syllabus requirements. In particular, it is important to check that the contents of this book match the syllabus that is valid at the time of entry.

- For candidates with special needs, a letter giving details should be attached.

- Theory dates are the same worldwide and are fixed annually by LCM Exams. Details of entry deadlines and examination dates are obtainable from the Examinations Registry.

- Submission of this entry is an undertaking to abide by the current regulations as listed in the current syllabus and any subsequent regulations updates published by LCM Exams / Examinations Registry.

- UK entries should be sent to The Examinations Registry, Registry Mews, 11 to 13 Wilton Road, Bexhill, Sussex, TN40 1HY.

- Overseas entrants should contact LCM Exams / Examinations Registry for details of their international representatives.

Examination Fee   £ _____

Late Entry Fee (if applicable)   £ _____

Total amount submitted: £ _____

Cheques or postal orders should be made payable to *The Examinations Registry*.
Entries cannot be made by credit card.

A current list of fees is available from the Examinations Registry.

This entry form should be sent to our NEW ADDRESS below:

The Examinations Registry
Registry Mews
11 to 13 Wilton Road
Bexhill, E. Sussex
TN40 1HY

Tel: 01424 22 22 22
Email: Mail@ExamRegistry.com